To: _____
_____

From: _____
_____

~~~

You are invited to share your cherished pearls by writing them on the pages provided.

An Enduring Gift

Mother's Pearls

Barbara Young

Copyright © 2023 Barbara Young

BYoungBooks.com

All rights reserved worldwide. This publication may not be reproduced in whole or part, stored or transmitted in any form or by any means – electronic, mechanical or otherwise – without written permission of the publisher, except to review or quote brief passages with proper citation.

This publication is based upon actual life events and experiences of the author and her mom. Any mention is oriented to their lives. The author acknowledges that common knowledge and geography change over time. No medical, nursing, psychological, financial, legal or other professional advice given or implied, nor any affiliation or financial interest established with any organization or product. Please seek your own professional advice as needed.

The only brands, product names, trademarks, or copyrighted material herein are property of the author, including *The Snoopie Law of Happiness*, *Mother's Pearls: An Enduring Gift*, the quoted pearls, and text.

All references and links were active and referred to active websites and related information at the time of first printing.

Third party sales of new and used copies are not guaranteed for quality, authority, or access to any additional benefit or content.

Cover Art by Samiullah Sahito

Interior Art by David Loofbourrow

Book Design by VivoDigitalArts

Editing by Anna Hourihan, Julie Beyers

ISBN 978-1-7330269-5-6

Printed in the USA by Ingram Spark

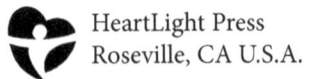

HeartLight Press
Roseville, CA U.S.A.

My Precious Momma,

You gave me a lifetime of wisdom, wit, and wonder. This book is another dream come true.

Gosh, I'm a Lucky Daughter!
Love, Barbara

It takes time to cultivate the exquisite, whether a pearl or a person. Pearls symbolize the beauty and value that can grow from the grit of life.

As I grew into a woman, I gathered my mom's loose collection of precious pearls—bits of wisdom, wit, and wonder—and strung them with those I cultivated.

They continue to bring grace into my life. When I *wear* them, I feel their resonant glow from within myself.

Real pearls improve from *wear*. The ones you live by, and those you give to others, will increase in value.

I imbue the pearls I share in this book with love and pass them on to inspire you to cultivate pearls for your strand.

∽∞∽

pearls

Timeless treasures made from something ordinary into something magical.

My college friends may have laughed at how crazy it sounded, but after a few years of hearing me say, "I'm going to live in the Caribbean one day," they believed it, too.

In our senior year, they dedicated Billy Ocean's song, "Caribbean Queen" to me.

As a graduation present, I took myself on a Windjammer sailing trip in the Caribbean.

Years later, a friend reminded me of the first morning of that trip—as we stood on deck, I silently looked around and then said with certainty, "I'm going to live here one day."

Six years after that trip, I moved to the Caribbean.

"Keep your dream sacred while you dream it."

Grit
Something that intrudes and awakens the natural process in a living creature to create and nurture beauty and strength.

Mom had her own version of "grin and bear it". She had to bear the noise of others' opinions, particularly about her. She discovered that a smile in the face of adversity could bring beauty into the situation, while it made her feel stronger.

"Smile through the madness."

Natural

Rare, organic, and untouched.
These pearls develop in the wild,
free of human intervention.

Mom and I were looking for something to do one Saturday afternoon.

"Let's have a come-as-you-are party!"

"What's that?" I asked.

"It's when you call people on the phone and invite them to a party that starts now. The way they are dressed when you call is the way they come to the party."

We made a list of our friends, and I called them on the phone with the invitation.

After I finished, I went to get ready for the party.

Mom said, "The joke's on you!"

I was still wearing my purple two-piece swimsuit from playing at the neighborhood pool earlier that day, so that's what I had to wear to the party!

"Come as you are."

Water

Both fresh and saltwater environments nurture beautiful pearls, strikingly similar yet deliciously different.

The walk to my car after a hospital work shift was down a long sidewalk that coursed through several parking lots. The air that day was dry and hot, but the grass adjacent to the sidewalk was shaded by trees.

Impulsively, I kicked off my work clogs and pulled off my socks. The moment I stepped onto the soft, moist grass, I felt a magnetic pull draining the fatigue and weight of the work shift from my body.

A nurse colleague hooted from behind as he too sunk his bare feet into the grass. We bubbled with laughter like children.

We shared memories of childhood— stomping in rain puddles, jumping into a pile of leaves, and wading in the shallows at a beach—as we walked to our cars.

"Let nature nurture you."

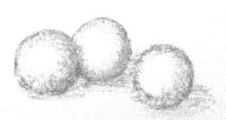

Cultured

Grown naturally, but human intervention facilitates the organic evolution into something exquisite.

Silence is often best, but I have found the words 'thank you' to be appropriate in a number of situations with awkward or tense moments. They give a dose of respect, permission to sigh, and an opportunity for each person to let go.

"Say 'thank you' if you must say something."

Authenticity

Real pearls may look smooth
but they have a gritty feel
when rubbed together.

In second grade I wore wide silver bands on my two front teeth. My classmates called me 'Silvertooth', which felt hurtful.

During show-and-tell, I told my classmates how fun it was to help my friend with his paper route. They thought that was cool.

I also told them how I tripped on a raised edge of the sidewalk, fell, and hit my front teeth on a concrete step. I described the horrific sound, and the sight of pearly white chips of my teeth laying on the step. They cried.

I shared how I held my mouth open for an hour while the dentist built my new teeth, and that I'd be wearing the bands for the rest of the year to make sure my new teeth were strong. They thought I was brave.

Their teasing helped me build confidence, and the kids found out I was real. The nickname stuck. Thereafter, when they called me 'Silvertooth', I felt their understanding and my courage.

"Names really can't hurt you, unless you let them."

Ocean

To an oyster, the ocean is the world.

In the mid-1980s, two friends and I planned to travel to Europe, including East Germany and East Berlin.

To this news, Mom said, "It's a big world and you're going behind the Iron Curtain? Maybe it will do you some good to know what it's like not to have any rights."

The Western European countries were interesting and the people friendly. There were no cell or GPS services then, so we used paper maps and people gave us directions. We experienced the cultures, learned to communicate in many languages, and ate new foods. We enjoyed the freedom of self-determination.

In distinct contrast were the scrutinizing checkpoints along the Eastern Bloc that were breath-holding.

They confiscated any travel guidebooks or information about the West. All our movements in East Germany and East Berlin were regimented and surveilled. The facilities at our assigned relief stops along the Autobahn were locked or gutted, so we used the nearby bushes.

The people in the East seemed inhibited. When passing on the sidewalk, they avoided eye contact with us, and were unreachable with a smile or wave. That was strange to me.

It was my choice to go there, but I didn't feel welcomed as a visitor. Then it entered my mind upon exiting East Berlin that it was possible they wouldn't let me return to the West. In this moment, my perspective shifted. I got it! The people wouldn't engage because they were afraid.

My mom wanted me to recognize rights versus freedom. Despite thinking I was free, in that moment I changed. I acted like I wasn't as I sat still, erect, face forward, even avoiding eye contact during the probing screenings and inspections. I felt vulnerable.

This adventure deepened my gratitude for my home and cultivated a broader experience of humanity.

"Maybe it will do you some good to know what it's like not to have any rights."

Depth

A pearl's unique luster results from reflected light. Deep internal layering magnifies it into an otherworldly glow.

Many times, in regretful retrospect, I've said, "I knew it!" But my inner voice and 'knowing' were too quiet. I couldn't hear them because of the noisy shoulds and shouldn'ts in my head.

I decided to start listening to these whispers. I learned to meditate, sink deep into my self-awareness, and reflect.

Learning about myself in this way magnified the whispers of insight from within so I could hear them and appreciate their value.

"Listen to the whispers."

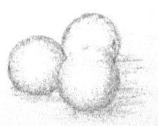

Harvest

Unlike an apple on a tree, a pearl becomes a pearl when liberated from within the shell.

After college, I started living by my own "Snoopie Law of Happiness": You should always have at least three things that you are working on.

    One that you're realizing soon.
    One that is in progress.
    And a third, just in case one falls through.

    I still live by this. It is part of my formula to live the life I imagine.

"You have to have a dream, if you want your dream to come true."

Nacre

To make a pearl, the creature layers its internal iridescence around a piece of grit.

I don't keep a list of losses, challenges or times I missed the mark. I can remember most of them, but I stopped carrying that baggage.

Through forgiveness, I let go of the pain and disappointment from a relationship with a wonderful guy who chose alcohol over us. With courage, I apologized to my friend whom I disappointed during a time when I was so stressed I was not myself. I released my regret for not leaving a very good paying but toxic job soon enough to preserve my wellbeing.

All of these have shaped my internal multi-dimensional structure. With self-reflection, I now see the hidden opportunity, lesson or gift in each adversity as purposeful changes to my life-path. Rather than reflecting pain, I now emit relief back into the world.

Mom called this the intricate weave of life. Instead of staying a victim, as I re-integrate myself into every situation, I claim my life as my own. With time, the beauty runs deeper, and I feel a glow emerging within.

"Weave it in."

Hardness

A pearl is an enduring treasure. Its toughness is less about hardness and more about wearability.

In my first big relationship, I thought love meant holding on.

I had a poster in the living room of my apartment with poetic words about setting something free if you love it. He pointed to the poster, and that's how I learned he wanted me to let him go. The poster also said if it comes back, it was yours. He never came back.

Even though done out of love, my tight hold on the relationship broke it.

I've learned the hard thing about love—its strength is not in holding, but in letting go. It's more wearable when each person in a relationship allows the other to evolve.

"Love is strong but gentle."

Durability

Soft, yet durable because they resist chipping, pearls improve with proper wear, which helps them shine.

I've learned to maintain my luster through self-care, purpose, and adventure. These needs are not the same for everyone.

The best latitude for my attitude is in the tropics, on a 21-square mile island. Because of my desire for adventure, I traveled as a nurse, and realized I could live, work, eat, sleep, and play anywhere in the world. So why not in the Caribbean? I made that choice.

Living in the Caribbean strengthened my vitality and the lifestyle made me resilient. Amidst the fresh air, moisture, sun, and the sea, I enjoyed another highly sought commodity—time. Time to work, create, play, and relax.

To build my home, I cleared and terraced my property, carried wood, mixed cement, painted, and learned about solar power. I worked as a nurse in the emergency clinic, and created my own Wellbeing practice and an architectural stained glass business. I also snorkeled, sailed, and danced to the music of live local bands in the open air. For me, it wasn't about doing nothing; it was about doing what I needed and what I wanted with my time. Stress was an enemy in this no-problem Caribbean lifestyle.

Frequently visitors to the island would come to the clinic asking for a medical note advising them not to fly. This meant they would have to extend their stay on-island by doctors' order. We locals understood there was magic at this latitude that made people feel their best and they wanted to enjoy it longer.

Once, a man stood at the nurse's station drumming his fingers. "Can I get a medical note?"

I said, "Ah, how much longer would you like to stay on-island?"

He said, "I don't want to stay longer. I want to leave early."

This sounded concerning, so I asked about his symptoms.

"Oh, I'm not sick. I've seen the beaches, snorkeled, and hiked to the petroglyphs. I've done it all. I'm bored and want to leave."

I happily wrote that note for him. He was not at his latitude.

"Take care of yourself. Others will be drawn to you because you aren't needy."

Surface

In light of a pearl's shine and glow,
a few superficial imperfections
simply become character.

My first pimple appeared on school-picture day in fifth grade.

I hardly noticed the red bump in the middle of my chin. Nor did I fret about getting a picture taken.

But just before it was my turn, one student said, "Ewww. You're going to get your picture taken with that Cyclops eye on your chin?"

Despite feeling uncertain, I flashed my dimpled smile on cue.

The photographer said, "You have a million-dollar smile!"

At home, I told Mom what happened. She said the photographer was smart because he knew a smile was the surest way to increase my face value.

"A smile is the glow of your heart worn on your face."

shape

A perfectly round, flawless, natural pearl is a rarity, but it's not the only one that is beautiful and valuable.

My friends and I are not all the same. Each is a lovely variation to the cliché of a perfectly round pearl.

Though we are well-rounded in knowledge, emotional durability, and integrity, we may be oval, pinched or lumpy like the mesmerizing and perfectly imperfect gems of the sea known as Baroque pearls.

What an amazing collection of gems we are!

"You get to pick your friends, but don't pick them apart."

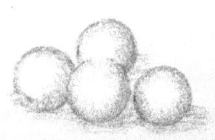

Color

Pearls come in colors ranging from classic to unique.

One has a fire-like iridescence, and another, a subtle soft cream glow. Several are mysterious Tahitian black, along with a few other salty beauties of the South Seas.

This is my rainbow of friends.

"The colors of a rainbow do not begin or end, they share with each other."

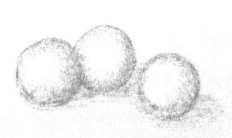

Overtone

Subtler hints of color that dance from within and around that give a pearl its character.

I remember the first time I got to clean a window.

As an energetic 7-year-old, I was stuck inside because it was a rainy and cold day outside. I kneeled by the living room window, chin on my folded arms, which I rested on the sill. As I gazed through the window and yearned to play outside, my warm breath streaked across the window.

Mom joined beside me and huffed her breath onto the window. Then she drew a heart in it with the tip of her index finger.

I huffed and drew a smiley face.

We giggled, told stories, and continued drawing cars, trees, and rainbows until the window was so smeared we couldn't see through it.

I said, "Oh no, we made a mess."

Mom said, "Yea, but it's a happy mess!"

She made it fun and easy to clean up.

"Attitude makes the difference between a breakdown and a breakthrough."

Quality
The fine-ness of expression of inherent characteristics.

After a relationship break-up, I usually wondered what went wrong or why I wasn't good enough.

Mom's guidance helped me see that these questions made me wish I was more like what another person wanted me to be. I was seeking the wrong thing by asking the wrong questions.

As I developed my interests and talents and expressed more of what I valued, I became more authentic, and when I did, my relationships significantly changed. I met people who were more like their true selves.

Then, finally, I met the one I wanted to meet, who wanted to meet me!

"Make yourself into the person you'd want to meet if you were the person you want to meet."

Transparency
Ability to clearly let light shine through.

Mom had a phrase she said to me as a child when she felt I wasn't being honest. It meant, 'I love you and I don't want to hurt you, but I have to tell you something that you may not want to hear.'

She was more interested in understanding the problem than getting mad. She wanted me to learn how honesty can help solve the issue, and we could work on it together.

Decades later, a friend and I used this method. We realized that often the hardest part was being honest with ourselves, in order to be honest with each other.

When you can't see something clearly, you need some light.

"Shine some love on it."

Translucence
Diffusion of light into various patterns and colors.

After nursing school, amidst the challenge of learning my first job, I felt disheartened.

"Mom, there are no more milestones in my life."

"What do you mean?"

"As a kid, there are all these milestones. You go to kindergarten, grade school, high school and college, and get a job. But then what? Get married, get a house, have kids? Is that all I have ahead of me?"

"Oh, Sweetheart. I am so excited for you. There are many milestones ahead in your life."

"There are? What are they?"

"Anything you want. You get to create them!"

"You get to create the milestones in your life."

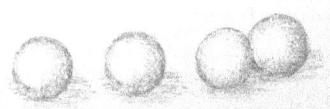

Luster

Captivating crispness and purity
of light that glows from within
a pearl expressing its value.

Three years into my nursing career, I also opened my Wellbeing practice for stress management. The nursing work was rewarding, but often the busyness and seriousness were fatiguing. Teaching meditation and providing therapeutic massage for others rejuvenated my soul. I became full of gratitude for having found this beneficial work.

Soon after, at a yoga meditation retreat, the facilitator had everyone surround me and reach with their palms toward me to observe and experience what he called my radiance. He said it was common for one's vibration to elevate and well-being to increase when they do massage because of the energy and discipline involved.

My thankfulness is what I felt radiating from me.

"Be thankful and you will sparkle."

sheen
The smooth shine of a pearl.

In third grade, I was the only girl in the energetic and rambunctious unofficial all-boys club in our neighborhood. Mom reminded me often to "be sweet." She wanted to teach me the importance of the tone of my voice. She said, "Even when you have something tough to say, you can say it nicely."

I have found that feeling thankful while speaking warms the tone of my voice. Especially when angry, it diffuses that emotion into a more meaningful communication. This is important because, as Mom taught me, "Nothing is so bitter as the words you regret saying."

People often mention that I have a soothing and caring voice.

"Always speak like honey is coming from your mouth."

Iridescence

The intricate display of color from within a pearl resulting from its multi-layered inner surfaces.

Since my childhood, when my best friend and I free-danced to her older sister's rock and pop albums, I have loved the feeling I get when I dance.

When I move in synchrony with meaningful words, rhythm, and melody, I lift out of sluggishness, shift from being stuck, and get back into my flow when lost or overwhelmed.

That fluid and open-hearted sense is a guide for creating health and joy for me. It leads me to activities and choices that make my true colors shine.

"Dance through life."

Reflection

The bright visual return of light after it bounces off the shiny inner surfaces of a pearl.

During my dating years, I learned to take time for myself between relationships. This took a conscious effort, especially when I moved to an island where the ratio was four men to one woman.

Taking time after a relationship allowed me to better understand myself and the relationship. I learned this through self-reflection and by returning to my values while single. This cultivated more coherence within myself. Then I naturally reflected a clearer image of myself when I met people. It also became easier to decide if I was ready for a relationship and with whom.

"Take time between relationships to get back in touch with yourself."

Refraction

Multi-angular redirection of light from the deep layers within a pearl that radiates its beauty outward.

I learned from my mom that being a parent less obviously involves letting go in love.

She had to release her protective embrace to allow my first step as a toddler, and let me leave the nest to go to kindergarten.

As I grew more curious, she was there for me to return to and rely on.

I remember the first time when I knew she was letting me go.

She anguished to accept that she could not provide for her growing child with her secretarial wage. I needed bigger shoes, and I had already worn hers out. This was difficult for us both, but thankfully, I could go live with my father. She had to let me go, and I had to let go of her.

Life got gritty as a preteen, as I changed schools and families.

Mom had given me sturdy roots. She taught me to take the sweet with the bitter and pearl-ize *the difficult times with beauty. So, I survived my first crush, first pimple, and moving into my first apartment. I became a nurse, traveled, loved and lost, and built my home in the Caribbean.*

My mom was always there for me through letters, phone calls, visits, and in my heart.

Later, when Mom faced dementia, the roots she gave me were my stability from which I could support her. Even as her cognition slipped and her body weakened, I witnessed her courage and beauty. The luminescence of Mom's wisdom helped me release her to find wings and transition from this world.

*"I gave you roots,
I give you wings."*

Coherence
The overall uniformity of individual, unique pearls.

Mom and I walked into a theater just before the movie was about to start. We noticed the density of people who filled most of the seats just before the lights dimmed.

I walked behind Mom as she took her time on the carpeted and terraced rows that led down to some open seats. She mis-stepped and dropped to her knees gracefully.

The audience gasped aloud.

Common to Mom's childhood and early in mine, theaters showed a funny cartoon before the start of the featured movie. Since this was no longer done, she felt she was the entertainment.

Mom started laughing as she gathered herself to stand. She sputtered, "There will be no cartoon prior to today's movie."

The audience met her in her humbleness and joined in her laughter. Grace came through this coherence and lifted her from embarrassment. She bowed to their applause.

"Always — remember grace."

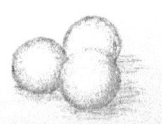

strand

Strength is in the common thread that connects unique individual pearls to form a brilliant unity within a whole strand.

I stood and watched five effervescent women talking and laughing—an executive, an investor, a motorcycle sales rep, a nurse, and a draftsperson. Each unique, yet so in unison. I felt a deep love for each of them as I remembered how I met each one.

Then I marveled at them all being together, meeting for the first time. They were from different parts of the world, different parts of my life. A tear came when I realized their connection was through me.

*Friendship is beautiful.
Love is the thread.*

"If someone is mean, they may need a friend and are afraid you won't be one to them. Be a friend."

As I wrote Mother's Pearls, I realized that each of my mom's pearls was a grit planted into my being through her guidance. My actions and way of living from these pearls create unique internal intricacies that allow light in. These reflect and refract that light of love and beauty into the world through me.

Every iridescent being impacts the world, in their own way, based upon the qualities of their inner light and resulting glow.

You need no polishing or cutting to be perfected. Because the wisdom of life is within you, you only need to let your inner light shine.

You are a pearl.

Namasté

The Pearls

7 - Pearls
"Keep your dream sacred while you dream it."
13 - Grit
"Smile through the madness."
19 - Natural
"Come as you are."
25 - Water
"Let nature nurture you."
31 - Cultured
"Say 'thank you' if you must say something."
37 - Authenticity
"Names really can't hurt you, unless you let them."
43 - Ocean
"Maybe it will do you some good to know what it's like not to have any rights."
51 - Depth
"Listen to the whispers."
57 - Harvest
"You have to have a dream, if you want your dream to come true."
63 - Nacre
"Weave it in."
69 - Hardness
"Love is strong but gentle."
75 - Durability
"Take care of yourself. Others will be drawn to you because you aren't needy."
83 - Surface
"A smile is the glow of your heart worn on your face."
89 - Shape
"You get to pick your friends, but don't pick them apart."
95 - Color
"The colors of a rainbow do not begin or end, they share with each other."
101 - Overtone
"Attitude makes the difference between a breakdown and a breakthrough."
107 - Quality
"Make yourself into the person you'd want to meet if you were the person you want to meet."
113 - Transparency
"Shine some love on it."
119 - Translucence
"You get to create the milestones in your life."
125 - Luster
"Be thankful and you will sparkle."
131 - Sheen
"Always speak like honey is coming from your mouth."
137 - Iridescence
"Dance through life."
143 - Reflection
"Take time between relationships to get back in touch with yourself."
149 - Refraction
"I gave you roots, I give you wings."
157 - Coherence
"Always – remember grace."
163 - Strand
"If someone is mean, they may need a friend and are afraid you won't be one to them. Be a friend."

Tribute

Author with her mom, Olive Marie

Favorite Color: Purple

Favorite Movie: 'The Sound of Music'

Favorite Poet: Kahlil Gibran

Favorite Song: 'You are My Sunshine'

Favorite Music: Big Band, and Country

Favorite Activity: Walking, talking with people, bargain shopping, driving and traveling by car.

Personal life lesson: "I have a right to be right and I have a right to be wrong."

Slogan: "Live life loving and be happy."

Greatest Joy: "My precious babies."

Remembered for: Her beautiful smile and open heart.

Your online reviews are appreciated.
They support the organic popularity
and availability of this
independently published book.

For interviews, keynotes, presentations,
book clubs, and readings—or other
inquiries—I would love to hear from you!

Find my blog, written works, and
contact information at:

BYoungBooks.com

Other Works by Barbara Young

Children's Picture Books

Grandma Lost Cuddles!
From the *Adventures with Dementia* series

Non-Fiction - Inspiration

The Heart That Rocks Health Care: Nurses, Move From Stress to Success, Empowerment, and Influence

Gift Books - Inspiration

Mother's Pearls: An Enduring Gift

Photography

Buddha Garden
Oyensbierg

Short Stories

Published in anthologies by Northern California Publishers & Authors 2019–present

www.ingramcontent.com/pod-product-compliance
Lightning Source LLC
Chambersburg PA
CBHW042358070526
44585CB00029B/2976